COPYWRITE 2021

SUP and CUP

**(A romantic cup of divine wine,
{white, rose or red}
is always a nice accompaniment
to a scrumptious
romantic sup)**

If you have been impacted by Covid19 and can no
longer afford meat every night, I have news for you…

Eating meat every night is not only unnecessary, it is detrimental.
Excess protein overtaxes your digestive system and puts a
strain on your intestines.

So…

If you can only afford 1 or 2 mainly meat meals a week… guess what!!
You are doing the perfectly right thing by your body and
you will be healthier and better off for not overeating meat….

You're OK.
You are supposed to eat like a pauper.

Eat up. You're doing great!!

HOLIDAY MEALS

FRENCH CRETON (Kreh-tuhn) To snack on over the Holidays

1 lg fresh pork shoulder
2 lg onion
2 tspns spike
1 cup water
1/2 tspn cinnamon to taste
1/2 tspn clove to taste
1 can evaporated milk
1 pkg instant potatoes

Remove the skin and fat from shoulder with a sharp knife

Put the skin fat side down in large saucepan
Cook the skin on low till the fat is melted (do not brown) then
Discard the skin

Cut the meat into large chunks
Put the meat into the melted fat

Add to the meat in the saucepan:
1 lg onion diced
1 tspn spike
1 cup water

Cook these ingredients on low until the meat falls apart (4 hours)
Discard the fatty liquid

Refrigerate the meat overnight in a bowl

Remove the meat from the fridge and
Put aside a few chunks of meat to shred with a fork

Put the remaining cold meat through your food processor until it becomes a spreadable consistency

Shred the few chunks of meat you put aside with a fork

Put the shredded meat and the processed meat in a saucepan on low and
Heat the meat and mix it together

Add to the meat in the saucepan:

1 raw onion chopped fine
1 tspn spike
1/2 tspn cinnamon to taste
1/2 tspn clove to taste
1 can evaporated milk NOT sweetened condensed milk

Simmer this for 30 minutes approximately to reduce the liquid to a pasty consistency, stirring every 10 minutes

Add 2/3 – 3/4 cup instant potato (more or less to your desired consistency,) to the mixture AFTER it has reduced to a pasty consistency

Stir the Creton till the potato is evenly distributed and then
Spread the Creton in a Pyrex baking dish to cool

Cover the dish and
Cool it in the fridge for 2 hours

Divide the Creton evenly into smaller containers and
Freeze what you won't be eating right away

Spread the Creton on French bread and
Serve

CHRISTMAS

FRENCH MEAT PIE Christmas Eve

1 sheet pastry dough
1 lb ground pork
1/2 lb ground beef
1 pkg instant potatoes
1 med onion chopped
3/4 tspn allspice
1/4 tspn cloves

Combine the beef, pork, onion and 1/2 cup of water in a frying pan
Cook covered on low heat 2 hours to render fat and strain it to drain the fat

Add the allspice and cloves to taste

Make the potatoes and add 2/3 – 3/4 cup to meat (more or less to your desired consistency) and mix in evenly

Press this mixture into a Pyrex or Corningare casserole dish

Top this meat with the thawed pastry dough (cut to size of pan)
Brush dough with egg or milk and
 prick dough generously with a fork

Bake according to dough instructions then
Cook the pie an additional 1 minute under the broiler to brown crust (watch it closely so it doesn't burn)

Cool 10 minutes

Serve topped with ketchup

CHOCOLATE STREUSEL COFFEE CAKE Christmas morning

Batter:

1/2 cup of butter
1 cup of Lakanto sugar (low on the glycemic index)
2 eggs
1-1/2 cup of flour
1 cup of sour cream
2 tspns baking powder
1 tsp baking soda
1 tsp vanilla

Cream the butter and Lakanto sugar and add the eggs and sour cream
Mix the dry ingredients and add to the above and mix well
Mix the filling in a separate bowl

Streusel filling:

1/2 cup Lakanto sugar (low on the glycemic index)
1 Tblspn unsweetened cocoa
1 tspn cinnamon
3/4 cup walnuts (floured)

Put 1/2 of the streusel filling into the bottom of a greased bundt pan evenly
Pour 1/2 of the batter into the greased bundt pan on top of the filling

Add the last of the streusel filling on top of the batter evenly
Add the remaining batter on top of the filling and

Bake @ 350* for 1 hour

Cool and Serve

BABY WASHINGTON APPLE PANCAKE Supper Christmas Day

1 can/jar Apple pie slices
4 eggs
3 Tblspn butter
2 tspns Lakanto sugar (low on the glycemic index)
1 cup milk
1 cup flour

Preheat your oven to 450*
Mix the eggs, flour, milk and sugar
Beat 2 minutes

Heat 2 Tblspn butter in glass pie plate
Add the batter to the melted butter in the glass pie plate

Bake 20 minutes @ 450*

Puncture the pancake towards the end to break any bubbles that may form

Add the apple pie filling on top of the pancake evenly

Return the pancake to the oven and bake it another 10 minutes
Serve

NEW YEARS

FRENCH RAGU New Years Eve

6 Quart Crock Pot

3 med onions
3 med potatoes
1 lb ground beef
2/3 cup flour
2 tspns cinnamon
2 tspns cloves
6 hamhocks

Boil the hocks for 20 min in enough water to cover them
Drain them and toss the water out
add more water and boil the hocks for 1 hour
Don't discard this water

Meatballs: 1 lb lean beef
             1 tspn clove
             1 tspn cinnamon
             1 salt

Put the hocks, water and meatballs in a crockpot
Brown 2/3 cups of flour on medium heat (watch it or it will burn)
Add 1 tsp clove and 1 tspn cinnamon to flour - more or less to your taste

Make a paste using this seasoned flour by adding cold water a teaspoon at a time, stirring till it makes a thick paste and
Add the paste to the hocks in the crockpot and stir it in to distribute it evenly throughout the liquid in the crockpot

Halve the potatoes and
Add the potatoes and diced onion to the crockpot

Slow cook on high for 5 hours

Serve (when mashed with butter and Spike and topped with the gravy, the potatoes are yummy)
(The meat on the hamhocks is underneath the fatty layer – cut through it. There is only a little bit of meat, but the meat is prime…)

Buttered French bread is a nice accompaniment

EGGNOG FRENCH TOAST New Years morning

3 cups eggnog
1/4 cup butter
8 large Eggs
1-1/2 Oz. Rum
1/3 cups Lakanto sugar (low on the glycemic index)
1/2 cup powdered Lakanto sugar   "   "   "
1/4 tspn cinnamon
1/4 tspn nutmeg
Salt
1-1/2 tspn vanilla
1" thick slices of Croissant bread or Bagel bread or bread of choice

Beat together all of the above ingredients EXCEPT the bread
Grease a Pyrex dish with butter

Dip the French bread into the batter and arrange it in a Pyrex dish.
Pour the remaining batter over the top

Cover and soak the battered bread Overnight in your fridge

Bake @ 420* on the bottom rack in your oven for 25-30 minutes.

Remove the dish from the oven and place the French toast on a rack to cool slightly on your countertop

Serve with butter and dust lightly with powdered Lakanto sugar.

NOODLE PUDDING Supper New Years Day

1 lb egg noodles
6 eggs
8 oz. cream cheese
1 lb ricotta cheese
1-1/2 cups Lakanto sugar (low on the glycemic index)
2 tspns nutmeg
2 Tblspn cinnamon
1/2 cup melted butter

Mix all of the above ingredients EXCEPT the butter and noodles

Par boil the noodles for 3 minutes once your water comes to a rolling boil
 and add the noodles to the mixture distributing evenly

Pour melted butter into 9x13" glass baking dish distributing evenly
 and add the batter with the uncooked noodles in it and distribute evenly
Bake covered with tin foil @ 350* for 45 minutes
Uncover it and bake for 15 minutes more
Serve with a dollop of sour cream on top.

EASTER

KITCHEN SINK MUFFINS (my original recipe) - Preheat oven to 350*. Easter morning

DRY ingredients:

2 cups Wheat flour
4 cups White flour
2 cups Lakanto sugar (low on the glycemic index)
2 cups Brown Sugar
2 tspns Salt
2 tspns Baking Powder
2 tspns Baking Soda
2 tspns Cinnamon
1 tspn Nutmeg

WET ingredients:

1 cup Sesame oil
1 cup milk
1 cup Molasses
8 eggs - beaten

Mix all the dry ingredients together in an extra-large bowl

Mix all the wet ingredients together in a smaller bowl

Mix the dry and wet ingredients together in the large bowl

Add to the batter:

1 cup raisins
1 cup chocolate chips
1 cup coconut flakes
1 cup shredded carrots
1 cup walnut pieces - floured

1 can pineapple tidbits WITH the juice

Combine everything together very well
Grease and flour large muffin tins or mini loaf pan
Add the batter distributing it evenly in the tins or pans

Bake @ 350* for 45 minutes or until a knife comes out clean

Serve warm with butter

FRENCH CROQUE MADAME Supper Easter

Sauce:

1-1/2 Tblspn ea. butter and flour
3/4 cup cream
1/4 cup cream cheese
2 tspns chives
1/8 tspn ea. rosemary and thyme
1/8 tspn Spike. VERY LITTLE!!

Sandwich:

8 oz. Gruyere
4 slices Jewish rye bread
3 tspns fresh chopped chives
8 oz. ham slices
3 Tblspn butter softened
Whole grain mustard
2 Eggs

Heat the oven to 350* and set the oven timer for 1/2 hour to keep sandwiches warm when done grilling..

In a saucepan melt the butter and add the flour
Whisk in the cream till it's smooth
Cook this mixture, stirring constantly, till it's thick

Remove from the heat, stir in cream cheese, chives, herbs and spike and Mix till the cream cheese is melted and all the ingredients are combined
Keep the sauce on low heat

Shred the Gruyere with a grater

Spread 4 slices of bread with butter on one side

Spread 2 of the buttered slices of bread with some whole grain mustard on the other side from the butter
Top this slice with shredded Gruyere and a 2 slices of ham

Assemble the sandwiches and
Grill them till the cheese is melted and the bread is golden brown
Flip sandwiches and continue to grill the other side till golden brown

Put the sandwiches in the oven on a cookie sheet to keep them warm.

Fry 2 eggs.

Remove the sandwiches from the oven to individual plates

Top the sandwiches with the eggs, sauce and the remainder of the shredded Gruyere and serve warm.

GRAPE-NUT PUDDING Easter Supper Dessert

3 cups milk
1 can evaporated milk
1 tspn vanilla
3/4 cup grape nuts
3/4 tspn liquid stevia (low on the glycemic index)
1/4 tspn nutmeg
4 eggs
Pinch of salt

In a deep baking dish beat eggs and liquid stevia

Add the milk and vanilla and stir it in

Add the Grapenuts and nutmeg last and distribute the Grapenuts evenly in the bottom of the liquid

Set the baking dish in a larger pan containing 1" water

Cover the baking dish and place the whole thing into the oven on the rack second to the bottom

Bake @ 400* for 1 hour till a knife inserted into it comes out clean

Dust with nutmeg and cinnamon

Serve with dollop of real whipped cream

ANY DAY MEALS
(in alphabetical order)

Each recipe makes 2-4 meals. Freeze the remaining portions in plastic containers with a sealed lid for another night. Remove the leftovers from the freezer and defrost them on the counter on the morning you will be reheating the meal. Reheat the food in the Instant Pot once defrosted.

ALL INGREDIENTS ARE ORGANIC!! You can use conventional as well

AMERICAN CHOP SUEY

1 lb ground beef
1 lrg can fire roasted diced tomatoes (partially drained)
1 can Tomato paste
1 lrg onion diced
2 C egg noodles

Saute the onion until it's translucent
Brown the ground beef and mix it in with the onion
Put the meat and onion into your instant pot
Add the diced fire roasted tomato and tomato paste
Add the Italian seasoning to taste
Stir and cook the dish on medium heat for 1 hour

Cook your pasta on the stove the typical way and stir it into the crock pot just before serving.

If you cook your pasta in the crockpot there is a good chance it will be gluey.

BEANS AND RICE

1 pkg frozen brown rice
2 cans aduki beans
2 tspns minced garlic
2 bay leaves
1 Wellshire Farms Kielbasa
Shredded cheddar cheese for topping
Diced scallions

Put the rice and beans and garlic into your instant pot. Season them with cayenne to taste. Stir it in well. Add 2 bay leaves. Cook it on medium heat for three hours.

Cut the kielbasa in 4" pieces then halve those pieces lengthwise. When the beans and rice are done cooking, put the kielbasa on a broiling pan on a rack over water and broil for 5 minutes turn and broil for another 5 minutes on the other side.

Serve beans and rice topped with shredded cheddar cheese and scallions with the kielbasa on the side.

BEEF BARLEY SOUP

1 quart beef stock
1 C barley
1 pkg frozen mixed vegetables
1 lb chuck stew meat
Cornbread

Cut up and dredge the meat in flour seasoned with a bit of Spike (to taste)
Brown the meat in butter in a frying pan
Then put all the ingredients plus the meat into the instant pot
Cook on high for 3.5-4.5 hours or until meat is tender.
Serve with a corn muffin (see my Corn Muffin recipe)

BEEF STEW

1 lb chuck stew meat
1-2 russet potatoes
3-4 carrots
1 lrg onion
1 container Cream of Mushroom soup (24 oz.)

Dice and saute the onion until it's translucent
Dredge the meat in flour and Spike and then brown it in butter
Wash and cut up the vegetables and mix them into the meat and onion mixture
Put all of the ingredients into a 9"x13" glass Pyrex baking dish mixing in the mushroom soup
Cover the Pyrex baking dish with tin foil and then poke holes in the foil to allow steam to escape
Bake @ 400* for 2 hours
Serve with French bread

CHEESEBURGERS

1 lb ground beef
1 pkg Brioche hamburger rolls
Cheddar cheese slices - 2 slices per hamburger
Condiments of your choice
1 tomato sliced
1 avocado sliced
6 strips of bacon

Broil the 6 strips of bacon on a rack suspended over 1/2" of water for 15 minutes
Divide the ground beef into 2 halves and form each one into a burger patty
Place the patties onto a rack suspended over 1/2" water
Broil the patties for 8 minutes on each side
Drain the patties and place them on bun and top them with 2 slices of cheese, 2 tomato slices, 2 avocado slices,and 3 strips of bacon
Add your favorite condiments (mustard, relish and ketchup) (I also add mayo, yum!!)

Serve with a Brew. Enjoy!!

CHICKEN BBQ WINGS

4 lbs Bell and Evans Organic chicken wings @ WFM
1 bottle Schlotterbeck and Foss Garlic Teriyaki BBQ sauce

Place the wings/drumettes on a cookie sheet with a generous sheet of parchment paper under them.
Cover them with your choice of BBQ sauce (or Schlotterbeck and Foss Ginger Teriyaki BBQ sauce)
Cook them uncovered @ 400* for 1 hour

Serve them alone. Eat half. Refrigerate the remainder to have for lunch during the week.

CHICKEN BILOUTE (Chicken Northern Frenchman)

4 boneless skinless chicken thighs
1 qt chicken broth (Pacific or Imagine)
1 bunch celery hearts
1 lrg onion

Dice and saute the onion until it's translucent
Dice the celery
Put all of the ingredients into your instant pot and cook them on high for 3.5 hours

Remove the cooked chicken, let it cool a bit, dice it and return it to the pot.
Serve with a corn muffin (see my Corn Muffin recipe) or French bread

CHICKEN RICE BAKE

1 pkg frozen organic brown rice
1 container cream of mushroom soup
4 boneless skinless chicken thighs

Put the soup and the rice in a Corningware baking dish
Mix them together and place the chicken thighs on top
Cover the dish with a glass pyrex top
Cook it @ 380* for 1 hour
Serve

CHICKEN STEW

4 boneless skinless chicken thighs
1 pkg frozen mixed vegetables
4 sm boxes 24 oz cream of chicken soup
1 Hannah yam diced

Mix all of the ingredients together in a deep Corningware baking dish
Cover it and bake it for 1 hour @ 380*
Remove the chicken thighs and cool them a bit and dice them
Return them to the stew and stir them in
Serve with a corn muffin (see my Corn Muffin recipe)

CHILI W/BEANS

1 lb Natures Rancher grass fed organic ground beef
2 cans kidney beans
1 lrg yellow pepper
1 lrg onion (optional)
1 lrg can (28 oz.) Fire roasted diced tomatoes (partially drained)
1 can tomato paste
1 t chili powder
Spike to taste

Saute the onion until it's translucent
Brown the ground beef
Dice the yellow pepper
Add all the ingredients to the instant pot with the diced tomatoes and tomato paste and seasonings
Mix the ingredients together thoroughly (be careful, the instant pot will be full)
Cook everything on high for 3.5 hours
Serve with a dollop of sour cream on top and tortilla chips on the side

CHOCOLATE SACK

1 sheet pastry dough
8 oz semi-sweet chocolate
1/3 C shelled walnuts
2 Tblspns butter
Powdered Lakanto sugar

Thaw the pastry dough for 20 minutes
Heat the oven to 425*

On a floured board, roll the pastry to a 14" square
Place the chocolate, walnuts and butter in the center of pastry dough
Pull the edges together and twist them into a sack
Bake the sack on a baking stone for 20 minutes @ 425*
Remove it from the oven when the timer goes off and let it stand for 10 minutes
Sprinkle the sack with confectioner's sugar
Pull the sack apart with your fingers and enjoy!

COD/SWORDFISH

1/2 lb of fish - it's enough for 1 person

Bake the sweet potato tots on a cookie sheet with silicone baking mat on it according to the directions on the package and leave them in the oven to stay warm while you are broiling the fish
Place the fish on a rack above 1/2" of water
    A) Broil the codfish for 15-20 minutes without turning and then check for doneness (it should flake easily)
    B) Broil the swordfish dotted with butter 8 minutes per side
Serve the fish with the sweet potato tots

CORN MUFFINS

3 C flour
3 C corn meal
3/4 C Lakanto sugar (low on the glycemic index)
4 Tblspns baking powder
6 eggs
2-1/4 C milk
3/4 C melted butter
1 can 14.5 oz cream corn

Mix the dry ingredients together
Mix the liquid ingredients together
Combine the ingredients (including the butter) but do not overmix them
Let the batter sit for 10 minutes
Grease the muffin tins with more butter and fill them 1/2 of the way up with the batter
Bake @ 425* for 25 minutes
Serve it with your favorite dish

CREPES

4 eggs
1 pinch of salt
1 C milk
1 C flour

Mix all the ingredients together
Pour the batter into the frying pan (not a cast iron pan)
Swirl the pan until you have a thin covering of batter covering the entire inside bottom of the pan
Cook this crepe until it's golden brown on one side
Flip the crepe and cook other side till it's golden brown
Serve the crepe with your choice of filling or butter with real maple syrup drizzled over it or with powdered Lakanto sugar sprinkled on top

GARBAGE CAN

1 lrg red pepper
1 lrg avocado
1/2 bag frozen sweetcorn defrosted
1 lb Natures Rancher grass fed organic ground beef (optional)
1 medium onion (optional)
1 container 16 oz WFM Thick and Chunky Cantina Style fresh salsa medium heat or your choice of salsa
1 pkg shredded cheddar cheese

Brown the ground beef if you are using it (if adding ground beef, then also add another 1/2 container of the salsa)
Wash and dice the fresh vegetables to bite size pieces
Mix all ingredients together with 1 container of Cantina Style salsa (1-1/2 container of Cantina Style salsa if adding the ground beef)
Serve it in individual bowls (dot the dish with 5-6 raisins {flies}) and serve each dish with tortilla chips on the side

GINGER GARLIC CHUTNEY

1 Apple
1/2 C raisins
2 oz. ginger root
3 garlic cloves
2-1/2 Tblspns lemon juice

Peel the ginger root
Put all the ingredients into your food processor and process everything till it becomes a chunky consistency
Serve the chutney with Carrs Wheat Crackers (or your own selection of crackers)

HARVEST SALAD (for 2) (my original recipe)

1/2 of a 3 oz. bin of Spring Greens
1 Avocado cut up
1 can sliced beets drained
1 handful chopped scallions
2 large radishes sliced thin
1 handful dried sweetened cranberries
1 handful chopped pecans
2 handfuls of croutons

Optional:
(2 chopped hard boiled eggs and crumbled bacon)

Drain the beets and put them aside
Wash and prepare all the other vegetables (EXCEPT the beets)
Then add them and the beets on top of the spring greens that have been divided into two bowls
Top the salad with cranberries, pecans and croutons (eggs and bacon, if desired) and your choice of salad dressing
Toss the salad and serve

HOT DOGS WITH SAUERKRAUT

2 hot dogs per person
2 Brioche hot dog buns per person
WildBrine red beet and red cabbage sauerkraut
Yellow mustard

Take the hot dogs and put them in a 2 quart saucepan with 1/4" water in it
Steam the hot dogs for 3-4 minutes after the water is boiling
Remove the hot dogs with a fork and place them into brioche hot dog buns
Top them with mustard and then
Top them with red cabbage and beet sauerkraut by WildBrine
Serve

LAMB CHOPS

3 rib or loin lamb chops
1/2 bag Sweet potato tots

Bake the sweet potato tots on a cookie sheet (with a silicone baking mat underneath them) according to the directions on the package and leave them in the oven to stay warm while you broil the lamb chops

Broil the lamb chops on a rack over 1/2" water for 6 minutes per side
Serve the chops with mint jelly and the sweet potato tots on the side
Easy peasy meal...

LASAGNA

1 pkg spinach and ricotta or 4 cheese ravioli
1 lrg can fire roasted diced tomatoes (28 oz) (partially drained)
1 can tomato paste
1 container 16 oz ricotta cheese
1 egg
1 Tblspns Italian seasoning
2 lbs of Natures Rancher grass fed organic ground beef or 2 lbs of ground mild Italian pork sausage
1 pkg shredded Italian cheese
Spike to taste

Brown the ground beef or sausage and put it aside
Drain the diced tomatoes and mix the diced tomatoes and tomato paste in a bowl
Beat the egg in another bowl and stir in the ricotta cheese and Italian seasoning and Spike to taste
Mix the egg, ricotta cheese and Italian seasoning and Spike together well

Assembly:

In the instant pot insert, cover the bottom with sauce and layer:

1) A single layer of the ravioli
2) A layer of 1/2 the ricotta cheese mixture
3) A layer of the ground beef or sausage
4) A layer of the tomato sauce
5) A layer of shredded Italian cheese

Repeat until you finish all the ingredients (they will just fit in the instant pot insert)

Wipe up the spills on your instant pot and cover it with the instant pot top
Cover and cook the dish on medium heat for 2 hours
Not much to look at but tastes like the real thing
Serve

MAC N CHEESE

1 package 8 oz shredded cheddar
1 block 8 oz cream cheese
4 C egg noodles (uncooked)
1 stick of butter
1 can evaporated milk
1/2 C water or milk

Melt the butter in the instant pot and stir in the pasta to coat it with the butter
Dump in the evaporated milk and water

Add the package of shredded cheddar cheese and cube the entire block of cream cheese and add in and stir. Cook the dish on low for an hour, stirring thoroughly @ 20 minute intervals

Stir it thoroughly when it's done to blend in the melted cream cheese and…
Serve (very rich dish) the dish with a corn muffin (see my Corn Muffin recipe)

NACHOS

Lay out round tortilla chips on a cookie sheet
Top the tortilla chips with shredded Monterey Jack and Colby cheese or a Mexican Blend shredded cheese
Top the cheese with jalapenos, chopped tomatoes, black beans, diced onions, diced green peppers (if desired) and browned ground beef (if desired)
Bake the nachos @ 350* for 10 minutes
Serve them with guacamole, salsa and sour cream. Mmmm...

OMLETTE'N YOU WIN (my original recipe)

6 eggs
2 slices cheddar cheese broken up into medium pieces
1 tomato sliced moderately thick
1 Tblspn Bernaise Sauce (buy on Amazon.com)
1 Tblspn heavy cream
4 Tblspns heavy cream (yes, again…)
6 slices bacon

OMELET

Break your eggs into a medium bowl
Add 4 Tblspns heavy cream
Mix thoroughly

Broil your bacon till crispy

Pour mixture into a smaller frying or omlette pan that has melted butter in it on Medium Low heat
Put the cover on your omelet pan and monitor its progress
You may want to turn the omelet over (very carefully) if it doesn't cook thoroughly on top

Add bacon, cheese pieces and sliced tomato to your liking

Mix: 1 Tblspn heavy cream and 1 Tblspn Bernaise sauce

After you assemble your omelet, remove it to your plate and drizzle your sauce over the top to your liking

Serves 1 or 2

PISTACHIO BREAD

1 stick of butter
2/3 C + 2-1/2 Tblspns Lakanto sugar (low on the glycemic index)
2-1/2 Tblspns crème de menthe
1 Tblspn peppercorns ground
6 egg whites @ room temperature
Pinch of salt
1 C flour
1/2 C pistachios

Preheat the oven to 350*
Ground up the pistachios in your food processor (be careful to leave them somewhat chunky)
Butter and flour your loaf pan
Cream the butter and 1/2 of the Lakanto sugar
Beat in the crème de menthe and ground pepper
Beat 5 egg whites with crème of tartar, salt and 1/2 of the Lakanto sugar till they are stiff (adding crème of tartar, salt and sugar a little at a time.) (make sure there is NO yolk in the egg whites or they will not froth)
Fold the flour and 5 egg whites into the crème de menthe batter a little bit at a time (Fold but do not overmix)
Add two thirds of the ground pistachios
Turn the batter into the floured and buttered loaf pan
Bake 35-40 minutes @ 350* and then remove the loaf from the oven
Put the remaining 1 egg white plus 2-1/2 Tblspns of sugar into a food processor and whip it till it's frothy then stir in the remaining ground pistachios
Slit the tops of the breads down the middle lengthwise and spoon this frothy pistachio mixture into the slits
Bake 10-15 minutes @ 350*
Let cool and serve

PIZZA HOMEMADE

Buy 2 - 12" crusts @ WFM
1 can 14.5 oz of fire roasted diced tomatoes (partially drained)
1 can tomato paste
1 pkg Sliced pepperoni
Your choice of veggies (yellow pepper, mushrooms, onion)
1 pkg shredded Italian cheese

Put one crust on a 14" pizza pie pan and put it in the oven while the crust is frozen and cook it for 10 minutes @ 350*
Remove the defrosted crust from the oven
Mix together the drained fire roasted diced tomatoes and tomato paste in a medium size bowl
Spread this mixture on the pizza crust to the edges of the crust (just about)
Top the sauce on the pizza generously with Italian cheese (I use the whole pkg)
Layer the pepperoni generously on top of the cheese
Top the cheese and pepperoni with diced/sliced veggies (slice the mushrooms thick and dice the peppers)
Bake the pizza @ 425* for 20 minutes
Remove it from the oven and let it cool for 5 minutes
Serve

PORK TENDERLOIN

1 DuBreton plain pork tenderloin
Cosmos minced garlic
Parsley, basil and thyme

Cut 1" long shallow slits in the top of the tenderloin parallel to the sides
Using a spoon fill the slits with minced garlic using your finger to push it into the slit
Sprinkle the top of the tenderloin moderately with the 3 herbs
Put the tenderloin on the roasting rack over 1/2" of water
Bake @ 400* for 45 minutes
Serve the tenderloin with sweet potato puffs or a baked sweet potato topped with sour cream and butter (halved and baked for 1 hour @ 400* - coordinate the potato cooking time with the tenderloin's cooking time)
Serve

POT ROAST

2 lb chuck roast boneless
Two russet potatoes
4 carrots
1 large yellow onion
1 container of cream of mushroom soup
1 tspn each Parsley, Basil, Thyme
Spike to taste

Do NOT peel the vegetables. Wash them and cut them up into bite size pieces.
Dice the onion into 1" square pieces.
Put all the food into a deep Corningware casserole dish large enough to hold it.
Put the roast into the dish and surround it with all the vegetables.
Pour all the mushroom soup over the entire dish, and cover it with your Corningware top.

Bake it @ 380* for 2.5 hours. Serve with Buttered Italian Bread...

SAUSAGE AND PEPPERS

1 pkg DuBreton mild Italian sausages
1 lrg 28 oz can fire roasted diced tomatoes (partially drained)
1 can tomato paste
1 lrg yellow pepper
Italian seasoning to taste

Cut everything up into bite size pieces and put all the ingredients into the instant pot
Cook the dish on medium heat 3.5 hours.
Serve in torpedo rolls

SEAFOOD SCAMPI serves 2

8 Sea scallops defrosted
10 Peeled and deveined shrimp defrosted
Cosmos minced garlic
3/4 stick of butter
1 tspn each dehydrated parsley, basil and thyme
2 Cups of egg noodles

Put a 2 quart saucepan filled 2/3 of the way with water onto your stove top burner and heat it until it's boiling
Boil the 2 Cups of egg noodles in the saucepan of water for 10ish, or so, minutes or until the noodles are soft.
Defrost 8 sea scallops and 10 peeled and deveined shrimp
Drain the seafood well
Saute the seafood in 3/4 stick of melted butter in a large frying pan with 2 Tblspns Cosmos minced garlic on medium heat (about 4 minutes) or until the seafood is cooked (do NOT overcook your seafood or it will become tough)

Add 1 tspn each parsley, basil, thyme
Mix them into the seafood and garlic and butter

Cook the dish further on low heat for 1-2 minutes to marry the flavors while stirring everything together
Mix in the drained egg noodles and stir them into the mixture to coat them well with the butter, garlic, herbs and seafood
Serve with buttered garlic focaccia bread

SHEPHERDS PIE

4 servings instant mashed potatoes
1 lb ground beef
1 lrg onion
1 pkg frozen corn
1 pkg shredded cheese

Dice the onion 1" square pieces and saute them in the butter until they are translucent
Brown the ground beef and mix in the sauteed onions and season it to taste with Spike
Make the instant mashed potatoes according to the directions on the box (substituting heavy cream for the milk)

Assembly:

Cover the bottom of a 9"x13" glass Pyrex dish with all of the ground beef and onion mixture
Spread the frozen corn on top of the layer of ground beef and onions
Top the sweet corn with all of the mashed potatoes
Top the potatoes generously with shredded cheddar cheese

Bake ucovered @ 380* for 45 minutes
Serve

SHRIMP JAMBALAYA

1 Pkg frozen cooked brown rice defrosted
1 can 28 oz of fire roasted diced tomatoes (partially drained)
1 can tomato paste
1 yellow pepper
14 peeled and deveined shrimp
1 pkg spicy smoked sausage such as andouille (very spicy) or kielbasa (mildly smoked)
We prefer the kielbasa.

Put the canned tomatoes and the tomato paste into your instant pot, and add the defrosted rice to the tomatoes.
Dice and throw in that pepper.
Add the sausage (sliced) and stir everything together well.
Cook the dish on high in your instant pot for 3 hours.
Add the uncooked shrimp and stir them in for the last 20 minutes.
Serve the dish with Ritz Crackers or equivalent...

SPAGHETTIS ET BOULETTES DE VIANDE for 4

SPAGHETTI AND MEATBALLS (The French way) (My original recipe for sauce)

Sauce

1 lg can 28 oz Fire roasted diced tomatoes (partially drained)
1 can tomato paste
1 jar pitted kalamata olives
1 yellow pepper chopped
6 oz. mushrooms sliced thick
1 Tblspn Italian seasoning to taste
2 tspns minced garlic

Place all of the above EXCEPT the kalamata olives into a 3-quart slow cooker

Cook on high for 3 hours

Add the kalamata olives the last 1/2 hour of cooking ONLY - only to warm them (or the olives will make your sauce taste bitter)

Meatballs – makes 12

1 lb ground beef or bison
2/3 C (more or less) of Italian flavored breadcrumbs
1 beaten egg
1-1/2 tspns minced garlic
2 tspns Italian seasoning
1 bottle red wine

Mix all of the above ingredients together well (EXCEPT the wine) and form the ground beef mixture into balls approximately 1-1/2" in diameter (you should be able to make 12 meatballs)

Place the meatballs in the bottom of a roasting pan that has 1/2" of wine in it.

Bake the meatballs in the wine @ 400* for 20 minutes
 turn and bake them for another 20 minutes on the other side

Serve the sauce over the pasta and top the sauce with the meatballs (I favor wide egg noodles)
Top your dish with Romano cheese and pour each of you a glass of the leftover wine.

STEAK WITH BERNAISE SAUCE

1/2 lb steak per person

Broil the steak under your broiler for 8 minutes per side for Organic Grass Fed Beef Ribeye or your choice cut of steak

OR:

Broil the Bison steak for 3-4 minutes per side for Organic Bison Ribeye or Bison Sirloin

Serve the steak with your choice of potato and sour cream with
Bearnaise Sauce on the side to dip your steak in.

STEAK, EGGS AND BEANS

Follow directions for steak above
Heat up your beans in small saucepan before you cook the steak
While the steak is cooking fry two eggs

Put the fried eggs on top of your steak and serve it with the beans on the side

STUFFED MANICOTTI

Buy a box of manicotti and follow the directions on the back Almost any recipe will do if you use organic ingredients.

Barilla Manicotti's recipe is pretty good, however, where it calls for sauce, I use my Spaghetti Sauce Recipe (previously mentioned under my Spaghetti and Meatball Recipe,) and leave out the peppers and mushrooms...   or not...

Season your Ricotta mixture with 1 tspn each of Parsley, Basil and Thyme and add a little Spike Seasoning to taste. (Be careful because the Spike is salty, and it doesn't take much...) Cook the stuffed manicotti according to the directions on the box
Serve

TEMPEST SEAFOOD CHOWDER (my original recipe)

2 C heavy cream
1 bottle clam juice
6 peeled and deveined shrimp
6 sea scallops cut in half
12 steamer clams or 12 little neck clams withOUT the shells
1 large Hannah yam
1 large onion
butter
dill

Saute the onions in the butter till they are translucent

In a 3 qt. slow cooker, add the cream, clam juice, diced sweet potato and sauteed onion

Cook these ingredients on high for 3 hours

Make a roux in a saucepan with some of the chowder liquid
When the roux is thick and smooth, add it to the slow cooker stirring it in to distribute the roux throughout the liquid evenly and
Cook the liquid for another 45 minutes to thicken it

Also add the shrimp, scallops and clams and let them cook in the slow cooker for the last 20 minutes

Top individual bowls of chowder with a pat of butter and sprinkle it with white pepper and dill to taste

Serve with a warm, buttered corn muffin (see my Corn Muffin recipe)

THE DEVILS RAIN CLOUD (with Silver Droplets)

Make a Chocolate Cake (any recipe)

Whip, sweeten and chill 3 cups of Heavy Whipping Cream

Cool the cake and frost it with the chilled Whipped Cream

Top the frosted cake with the candy silver balls

Serve and Devour...

TOP NOTCH CHICKEN (My original method)

A 4 - 5 pound chicken
Spike
Parchment paper

Wash the chicken inside and out and season the outside with Spike

Place an 18" piece of parchment paper over the chicken to make a tent (lay it right on top of the chicken from side to side, its ok if it touches)

Place the chicken with the parchment paper on it on a rack suspended over a roasting pan that has 1/2" of water in it.

Place the above on the second to the bottom rack in your oven

Bake @ 400* for two hours and
Enjoy the juiciest, most succulent chicken of your life...

WAFFLES ADMIRAL (my original recipe)

Toast 2 Belgian waffles (medium sized)
Butter them rather generously
Spread 1 with chunky peanut butter
And the other with Strawberry jam/preserves

Sandwich the 2 waffles together

Enjoy!!

SWEET TEA WISHES AND LOBSTER DREAMS

My palate aquiver
My dinner plates shiver
Gourmet delicacies
From deep in the sea

I'd eat this way each day
If I could
And not just only
if I should

Chilled lobster dipped
In melted butter
My heart and tummy
Both aflutter

Sweet tea to wash
The feasting down
Fit for a queen
Sporting a crown

I finish hence
The food is gone
My tummy once
Again forlorn

There's still a treat
That's left to eat
It's called dessert
And it's tout suite...

These poems are just for fun!! But the proceeds from the sale of my books are going to go in part to stopping the laboratory testing being done on companion animals.

BONE IN YOUR TEETH!!

DEAD END

IF YOU LIKED THIS BOOK, FEEL FREE TO ENJOY MY OTHER BOOKS.

An Emotional Wonderland
Blossoms in the Breeze
Dark O'Clock
Daydreams @ Midnight
Faerie Land
Heart and Soul
MoonDust
Simple Pleasure is Great Treasure
Without Measure
The Sky's Enterprise
AND OTHERS!!

Made in the USA
Middletown, DE
23 November 2023